Walt Disney's Comics and Stories
No. 670 July 2006.
Published monthly by Gemstone Publishing.
© 2006 Disney Enterprises, In., except where noted.
All rights reserved. Nothing contained herein may be reproduced
without the written permission of Disney Enterprises, Inc.,
Burbank, CA, or other copyright holders.

ISBN 1-888472-28-6

J 741.5
Wal

OHH-H, MISTER SMARTY PANTS! I FOUND YOUR— ♪♪

THANKS, PALLY!

GLOM!

HEY! WHAT...!

SLAM!

OH! HEARD ME *BASH* SCIENCE, EH? TRYIN' TO GET *EVEN?* WELL YOU CAN'T ROB *ME* OF MY REWARD!

OPEN UP! I *KNOW* YOU'RE IN THERE TESTIN' THEORIES!

BONK! DONK! BAM!

WELL, I *REFUSE* TO ACCEPT ANY *THEORY* THAT'S TOO *COMPLEX* FOR *ME* TO UNDERSTAND! AND WHAT'S MORE—

=GREEAAAGH! CHOKE! KOFF!=

SIMULATED CIGAR SMOKE! A *CHEMIST* TOO, EH? =SNORT!=

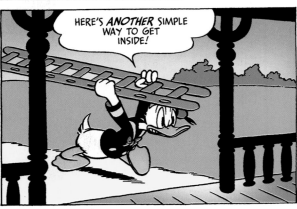

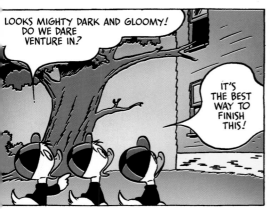

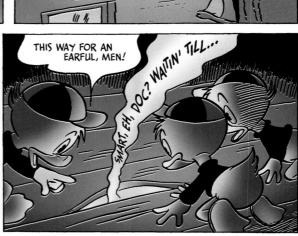

DOCTOR BROADMIND?... I HAVE HID DER FORMULA *RIGHT* WHERE YOU VANTED! JA! WHERE *NO ONE* VILL *EVER* FIND IT!...

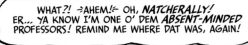

WHAT?! ⇒AHEM!⇐ OH, *NATCHERALLY!* ER... YA KNOW I'M ONE O' DEM *ABSENT-MINDED* PROFESSORS! REMIND ME WHERE DAT WAS, AGAIN!

IN DER *MOUTH* OF KOPFSTEIN DER P-SYCHIATRIST, SILLY! IN HIS *BIG STONE HEAD* ON SCIENCE PEAK!

OH, RIGHT! RIGHT!... NOW TELL ME *WHICH* HEAD DAT *IS*, BROTHER! IT...

HELLO? HELLO?

CLICK!

?

LINE'S GONE DEAD... OH, WELL! *C'MON*, SNOOKS! YOU COULD USE A VISIT TO TH' SHRINK, ANYWAY!

I *COULD?*

I'M *KIDDIN'*, DUMMY! WE'RE GONNA GO MAKE ONE O' THEM PETRIFIED NOGGINS SAY UNCLE!

CURIOUS! I *KNOW NO* KOPFSTEIN ON SCIENCE PEAK!... NOR *ANY* KOPFSTEIN WHO STUDIES THE BRAIN!

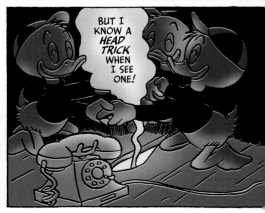

BUT I KNOW A *HEAD TRICK* WHEN I SEE ONE!

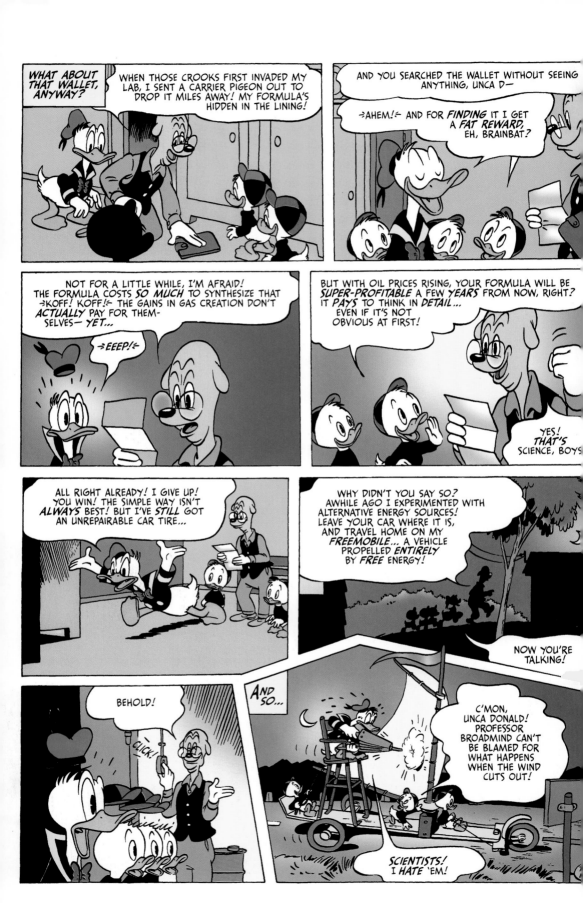

Walt Disney's

MICKEY MOUSE

PART **1** OF **3**

in

love trouble

ALMOST HOME, B'GAWRSH! WONDER IF ANYBUDDY KNOWS WE'RE A'COMIN'?

MINNIE DOES! I WIRED HER WHEN WE STARTED!

SHE'S ALWAYS SO TICKLED TO SEE ME BACK, I KNEW SHE'D WANTA MEET THE TRAIN!

YM 045

I ONLY HOPE SHE DOESN'T GET MUSHY! KINDA EMBARRASSING IN FRONT OF...!

HEY... WE'RE PULLIN' IN!

THAT'S FUNNY... SHE DOESN'T SEEM TO BE HERE! I DON'T UNDERSTAND...!

BURBAN

WELL, FER A GAL THAT'S SO GLAD TO SEE YUH, I'LL SAY SHE AIN'T **TOO** MUSHY!

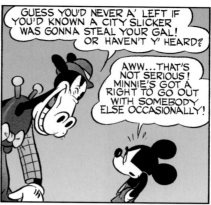

GOSH... ACCORDING TO HORACE AND CLARABELLE, MINNIE SURE SEES A LOT OF THAT NEW GUY! MAYBE, THOUGH, THEY WERE JUST KIDDIN' WITH ME!

AFTER ALL, JUST 'CAUSE HE CAN DANCE AND DO PARLOR TRICKS IS NO...

OH, GOOD MORNING, PATRICIA!

WHY, MICKEY! WHAT A SURPRISE! I HAVEN'T SEEN YOU IN AGES!

PERCY PIGG

NO, I'VE BEEN AWAY QUITE A BIT!

I SEE A LOT OF MINNIE! SHE'S EVERYWHERE IN THE SOCIAL WHIRL, SINCE SHE'S BEEN GOING WITH MONTY!

HE'S SUCH A CHARMING GENTLEMAN, I DON'T BLAME HER FOR... OH, DEAR ME... HAVE I SAID SOMETHING WRONG?

DEAR ME...I'M ALWAYS PUTTING MY FOOT IN IT! I SHOULDN'T HAVE PRAISED MINNIE'S NEW FLAME TO YOU!

THAT'S ALL RIGHT PATRICIA... MAYBE THE GUY IS OKAY...

...BUT A TWERP THAT JUST GOES DANCING AND PARTYING ALL THE TIME... WELL, THAT'S NOT MY LINE!

THAT REMINDS ME...I'M GIVING A LITTLE PARTY TOMORROW NIGHT! IF YOU'D CARE TO COME...?

PIGG

SAY... THANKS, PATRICIA! I'LL BE THERE!

HOT DOG! I'VE GOT THE JUMP ON MONTY THIS TIME!

MINNIE MOUSE

TO BE CONTINUED!

HOLD ONTO YOUR SEAT, DONALD! WITH MY NEW *POST-TEMPORAL RECORDER,* I'VE CAPTURED A *SOUND* FROM TEN SECONDS IN THE *FUTURE!*

DANGER IN DUCKBURG

A THRILLER

4-064

EADS UP! THOK!

HMPH! THAT COULD HAVE BEEN RECORDED *ANY* TIME!

HEADS UP!

THOK!

T DO YOU Y NOW?

THE ONLY THING *I* HAVE TO SAY IS "OW"!

THAT, AND HOW DO I *KNOW* YOU DIDN'T *SET THINGS UP* WITH THAT PAPERBOY? JUST TO *FREAK* ME OUT?

WHAT AWFUL *SCREAMS!* IT SEEMS SOMETHING *TERRIBLE* WILL HAPPEN HERE IN ABOUT TWO HOURS!

WHAT IF IT'S AN *ATTACK*, LIKE IN THIS *BOOK* I'VE BEEN READING?

DANGER IN DUCKBURG

A THRILLER

MAYBE YOU'VE RECORDED A GANG OF *CROOKS* DOING US *HARM*—AFTER HAVING [BR]OKEN IN TO *STEAL* YOUR INVENTIONS!

[A]ND WE *CAN'T CALL* [T]HE *POLICE* BECAUSE [IT] *HASN'T HAPPENED* YET!

[WE]'VE GOT [T]O *PROTECT* [O]URSELVES!

AND MY *LAB!*

I KNOW! I'LL CREATE A *MACHINE* THAT WILL SHOCK, PUNCH AND *CAGE* ANY INTRUDER!

[AB]OUT HALF [AN] HOUR [LA]TER!

⇥WHEW!⇤ NOW SET THE SPRINGS TO *23 POUNDS* PER SQUARE INCH!

DONE!

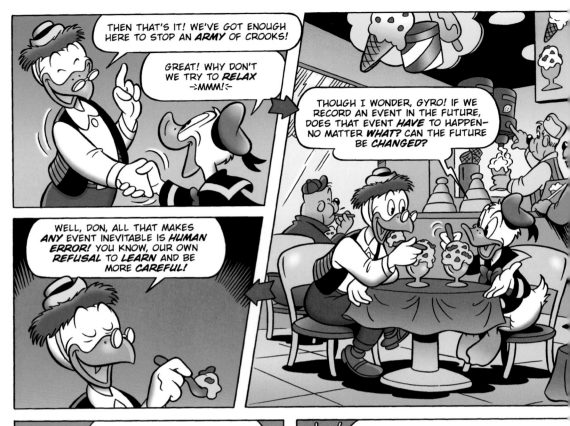

THEN THAT'S IT! WE'VE GOT ENOUGH HERE TO STOP AN *ARMY* OF CROOKS!

GREAT! WHY DON'T WE TRY TO *RELAX* ⇝MMM!⇜

THOUGH I WONDER, GYRO! IF WE RECORD AN EVENT IN THE FUTURE, DOES THAT EVENT *HAVE* TO HAPPEN— NO MATTER *WHAT*? CAN THE FUTURE BE *CHANGED*?

WELL, DON, ALL THAT MAKES *ANY* EVENT INEVITABLE IS *HUMAN ERROR*! YOU KNOW, OUR OWN *REFUSAL* TO *LEARN* AND BE MORE *CAREFUL*!

⇝HMMM!⇜ I REALLY WISH YOU HADN'T MENTIONED HUMAN ERROR!

BECAUSE NOW I CAN'T *REMEMBER* IF I S THE ALARM TO *23* POUNDS PER WHATEVER— *32* POUNDS! WILL THAT MAKE A *DIFFERENC*

A *DIFFERENCE?* 32 POUNDS COULD *JAM* THE SPRINGS AND RENDER THE ENTIRE SYSTEM *INOPERABLE*!

SO THAT'S A *BAD* THING, RIGHT?

YOU SET IT FOR *32* POUNDS! THE ALARM IS *ARMED*, BUT IT WON'T GO *OFF*!

OH, ME! SO WHEN THE CROOKS DO TURN UP, OUR BURGLAR STOPPER WON'T STOP THEM!

THIS SPRING IS JAMMED BADLY! GIVE ME A HAND! MAYBE WE CAN *LOOSEN* IT!

ON THREE, PULL WITH *ALL* YOUR MIGHT! ONE...TWO...

EEE! EEE! EEE! EEE!

YEEEBOICKS!

HELP! *HELP!* OH, *HELP!*

AGK! AGK! AGK!

NINE O'CLOCK! LOLO STARTING FOR THE BALL! AND I HAVE ALMOST NOTHEENG TO MY NAME!

AH, WELL! IT DOE NOT COST SOMETHEE TO **LOOK**!!

WELL, IF IT ISN'T JOE CARIOCA! WHERE'S **LOLO**, JOE?

AREN'T YOU GOING TO THE BALL, JOE? **MY**, WHAT WILL LOLO **SAY**!

SEE YOU LATER, MY AMIGOS! I'M **OFF** TO TH BA

Y, YOU DIDN'T
TAY LONG,
OE! DIDN'T
OU LIKE THE
PARTY?

I FORGOT
MY **MASK**,
THAT'S ALL!
GOING
HOME TO
GET IT!!

BETTER TAKE
A **CANDLE**,
JOE! IT'S DARK
IN THE PARK!

OH! OH!
A BANDITO
!!!

AH, **HA!**
COMES **JOE**
CARIOCA,
DEFENDER OF
THE PEACES,
EEN THE NEEK
OF TIME
!!!

REST EASY, SENOR! *I'LL* CATCH HIM FOR YOU!!

MY, WHAT AN **UNUSUAL** COSTUME!

YES— **STRIKING**!!

BUT, LOLO! YOU PROMISED **ME** THEES DANCE! EET EES A **SAMBA**!

NO! NO! SHE PROMISE **ME!**

AHEM! PARDON **ME**, GENTLEMENS!!

SENORES, LOLO HAS THEES DANCE WEETH **ME — JOSE' CARIOCA!**

DUCK TALES

BEFORE *THEY WERE* DuckTales

THE LOST CROWN *of* GENGHIS KHAN

LAND BENEATH *the* GROUND

ON SALE BEGINNING MAY 24TH 2006!

MICRO-DUCKS *from* OUTER SPACE

HOUND *of the* WHISKERVILLE

BACK *to the* KLONDIKE

LEMMING *with the* LOCKET

© 2006 Disney Enterprises Inc

GEMSTONE PUBLISHING

Did you know that some of your favorite *DuckTales* stories were created more than 50 years ago by one of the greatest Disney cartoonists of all times? Gemstone Publishing presents a collection of stories written by the legendary Carl Barks, originally published in comic books and then later adapted for the cartoon series *DuckTales*. See these wonderful adventures as they originally appeared and then go back and watch them animated!

Look for *Carl Barks' Greatest DuckTales Stories Volume 1* at your favorite comic shop or visit www.gemstonepub.com/disney. And look for Volume 2 this July!

CARL BARKS' GREATEST DUCKTALES ADVENTURES

ULP!

ARE YOU A DONALDIST?

on • ald • ism \ dän'-ld-iz'-em \ *n* : the research of Disney comics, and/or the fan culture that is found among Disney comics aficionados (Jon Gisle, 1973)

Go on, admit it. You like reading about comics history... but you love reading historically important comics themselves. You want a real Disney comics archival book—a thick trade paperback full of those extra-esoteric Duck and Mouse tales that just wouldn't fit in anywhere else.

You're a Donaldist! And we know where you're coming from.

Dive into the 160-page
DISNEY COMICS: 75 YEARS OF INNOVATION *for:*

- *Great Donald sagas by Carl Barks (a newly-restored "Race to the South Seas"), Don Rosa ("Fortune on the Rocks"), and Al Taliaferro (the seminal "Donald's Nephews")*
- *Never-before-reprinted Mickey tales by Floyd Gottfredson ("Mickey Mouse Music") and Romano Scarpa ("AKA Cormorant Number Twelve")*
- *Ducks by Daan Jippes, Dick Kinney, William Van Horn, and Daniel Branca*
- *Mice by Byron Erickson, César Ferioli and Paul Murry*
- *Renato Canini's José Carioca, Gil Turner's Big Bad Wolf—and Brer Rabbit too!*

GEMSTONE PUBLISHING *presents*
WALT DISNEY TREASURES VOLUME ONE
Available August 2006

(Any similarity between this book and the Disney DVDs you love to collect is purely intentional!)

© 2006 Disney Enterprises, Inc.

E

JOSÉ, BE CAREFUL! YOU WEEL FALL!

NOW, EEF YOU DON'T MIND WAITING, AMIGO, I AM COMING UP TO GET YOU!

WALT DISNEY Presents

The LI'L BAD WOLF

GEE, POP... I ALMOST WISH WE HADN'T COME UP HERE ON OUR VACATION!

NONSENSE, M'BOY! JEST BREATHE THAT CRISP FRESH AIR!

BESIDES, A FELLER LIKE ME *NEEDS* A VACATION! AFTER A BUSY YEAR O'CHASIN' AFTER THEM THREE LI'L PIGS, I CRAVES A REST!

I'M GETTING AWFULLY TIRED, POP!

BAH! YOU MODERN KIDS JUST CAN'T TAKE IT!

BUT IF YER REALLY SO TIRED, WE'LL CAMP HERE FER TH' NIGHT!

TH-THANKS, POP!

OKAY, SON! PUT UP TH' TENT, GATHER TH' WOOD, BUILD TH' FIRE, COOK TH' DINNER, AN'...

WHAT'N THUNDERATION WAS THAT?

A COYOTE, POP...THAT'S ALL!

GAWSH! HAVE I GOT TO LISTEN TO THAT HOWLIN' ALL NIGHT?

WHAT TH' DICKENS IS HE HOWLIN' ABOUT, ANYWAYS?

PROBABLY JUST A PAPA COYOTE CALLING TO HIS LITTLE COYOTE ...WELL...G'NIGHT, POP...ZZZZ

WERE YOU HOWLING FOR ME, PAPA BENT-TAIL?

I MOST CERTAINLY WAS, JUNIOR!

IT'S HIGH TIME YOU LEARNE TO GO OUT INTO THE WORLD AND RUSTLE FOOD FOR YOURSELF!

TONIGHT, I SHALL LET YOU GO OUT ALL ALONE AND GET YOURSELF A CHICKEN!

A CHICKEN?

OH, BOY! WHOOPEE! YA HOO!

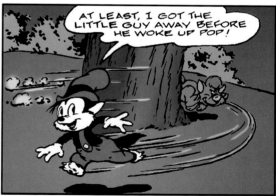

Walt Disney's DONALD DUCK in WHEELS ON FIRE

FORMULA ONE RACING IS AN EXPENSIVE BUSINESS! AND IT'S FILLED WITH UPS AND DOWNS! TEAM MCDUCK HAS HAD ITS SHARE OF THOSE! MOSTLY DOWNS...

UNCA SCROOGE *KNOWS* WE'VE GOT TO WIN THE RACE IN MONZA TO STOP GLOMGOLD FROM GETTING HIS MITTS ON THE GRAND PRIX CUP!

SO WHY DOES HE PICK *NOW* TO CUT BACK THE BUDGET?!

071

2-005

THAT TIGHTWAD LOVES TO PINCH A PENNY!

GRRR! IT'S PINCHED SO TIGHT WE CAN'T EVEN AFFORD A DECENT *TRUCK!*

LET'S JUST GET THERE IN TIME FOR THE START...

WAAK! TELL ME THAT *DIDN'T* JUST HAPPEN!

KA-GOOM!

KNEW IT WAS A MISTAKE TO TAKE A SHORTCUT ACROSS THE ALPS!

THERE'S NO PROBLEM WITH THE SHORTCUT! IT'S THIS *HUNKA JUNK!*

THONK!

HOW ARE WE GONNA FIND A MECHANIC IN THE MIDDLE OF *NO-WHERE?!*

TROUBLE, DEAR COUSIN?!

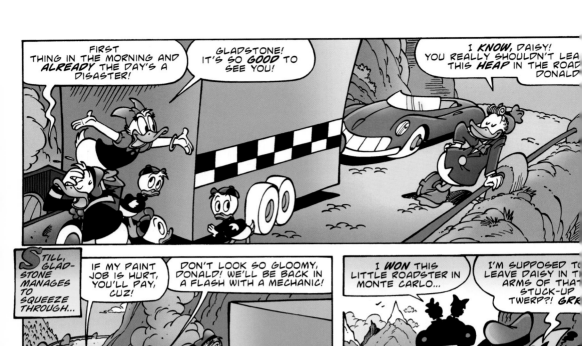

FIRST THING IN THE MORNING AND *ALREADY* THE DAY'S A DISASTER!

GLADSTONE! IT'S SO *GOOD* TO SEE YOU!

I *KNOW*, DAISY! YOU REALLY SHOULDN'T LEA THIS *HEAP* IN THE ROAD DONALD

*S*TILL, GLADSTONE MANAGES TO SQUEEZE THROUGH...

IF MY PAINT JOB IS HURT, YOU'LL PAY, CUZ!

DON'T LOOK SO GLOOMY, DONALD! WE'LL BE BACK IN A FLASH WITH A MECHANIC!

I *WON* THIS LITTLE ROADSTER IN MONTE CARLO...

I'M SUPPOSED TO LEAVE DAISY IN T ARMS OF THA STUCK-UP TWERP?! *GRR*

*S*OON, IN A SMALL MOUNTAIN VILLAGE...

THE ONLY GARAGE IN TOWN IS *CLOSED*!

THERE'S A SIGN! "GONE TO THE RACES IN MONZA!"

HM! I CAME UP HERE FOR A NICE QUIET BREAKFAST AND GET *AWAY* FROM THAT PESKY McDUCK TEAM!

GARAGE

I'LL GIVE UNCLE SCROOGE A CALL! GET HIM TO SEND A TOW TRUCK!

*B*UT... UNBELIEVABLE! THE CAFÉ OWNER SAYS A *LANDSLIDE* BROUGHT THE PHONE LINES DOWN!

SO WE'LL *MOTO* TO MONZA! THA WHERE SCROOG IS WAITING, RIGHT?!

MONZA

GOOD JOB, SIGNOR! THANKS FOR HELPING WITH MY LITTLE JOKE!

I DON'T GET IT! WHERE'S YOUR USUAL GOOD LUCK, GLADSTONE?!

HA! MY GOOD LUCK IS THAT I GET TO SPEND MORE TIME WITH *YOU*, DAISY!

A BREAKDOWN, EH? THAT'S WHAT *I* CALL GOOD LUCK! ANY TROUBLE FOR McDUCK IS WELCOME NEWS!

MEANWHILE! WHY DO YOU EVEN BOTHER, UNCA DONALD?! YOU DON'T KNOW ANYTHING ABOUT CARS!

I *HATE* WAITING! AND I'M *MAD!* AND *WHEN* I'M MAD...

THONK!!

I CAN DO *ANY-THING!*

WOW!

VROOOM!

SOON! GOOD THING WE DON'T NEED A GARAGE ANYMORE! IT'S *CLOSED!*

I WANNA KNOW WHERE THAT *IDIOT'S* TAKEN MY GIRL!

AHA! McDUCK'S HOT-HEADED DRIVER IS *JEALOUS!* THIS COULD BE FUN!

071

SAY, HOW WOULD YOU LIKE TO EARN A LITTLE *EXTRA?!*

AND SO... YOU SAY THEY PARKED UP ON THAT *MOUNTAIN?!*

SI, SIGNOR! THERE'S A ROMANTIC CAFÉ AT THE TOP!

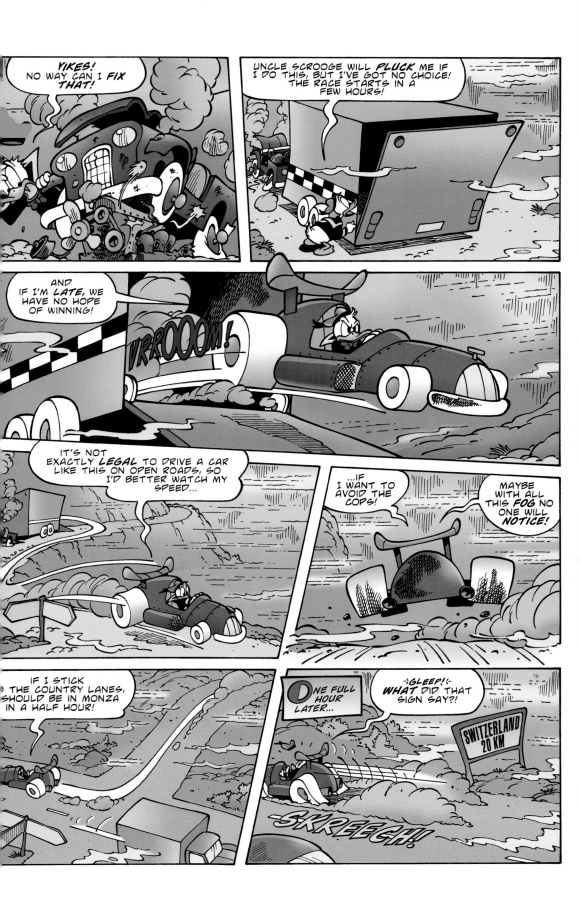

LATER, OUTSIDE THE RACE TRACK IN MONZA!

TSK, McDUCK! WE MISERS ARE OLD HANDS AT *SCRIMPING* ON TRANSPORTATION...

STIFLE IT, GLOMGOLD!

BUT SCRIMPING WITH NO *BACKUP PLAN?* IT'S RACE TIME, AND YOUR CAR'S NOWHERE TO BE —

SAY! WHAT'S *THAT?!*

WHEEE-OO! WHEEE-OO!

WEEE-OO! WEEE-OO!

DONALD!

NO!

SECONDS BEFORE THE START...

⇒GACK!⇐ THE CAR *STINKS* LIKE A PIGSTY!

NEEDS NEW TIRES, TOO!

AND THEY'RE *OFF!*

BAH! HOW DID THAT LAME-BRAINED DUCK *EVER* GET HERE IN TIME?!

RRROOARR!

HAW! THE ENGINE'S *ALREADY* WARMED UP!

VRROOOM!

GLOMGOLD'S DRIVER SURE IS *FAST* TODAY!

BUT UNCA DONALD IS *FLYING!*

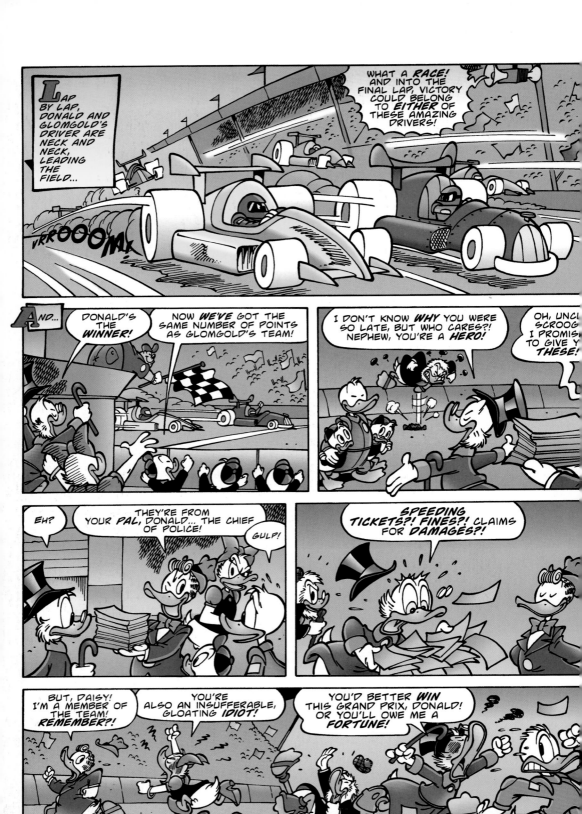